ELECTRIC RAYS MAKE ELECTRICITY!

BY LOUIS MALLORY

Gareth Stevens
PUBLISHING

Please visit our website, www.garethstevens.com. For a free color catalog of all our high-quality books, call toll free 1-800-542-2595 or fax 1-877-542-2596.

Cataloging-in-Publication Data
Names: Mallory, Louis.
Title: Electric rays make electricity! / Louis Mallory.
Description: New York : Gareth Stevens Publishing, 2024. | Series: Electric animals | Includes glossary and index.
Identifiers: ISBN 9781538292969 (pbk.) | ISBN 9781538292976 (library bound) | ISBN 9781538292983 (ebook)
Subjects: LCSH: Rays (Fishes)–Juvenile literature. | Electric fishes–Juvenile literature.
Classification: LCC QL638.8 M355 2024 | DDC 597.3'5–dc23

Published in 2024 by
Gareth Stevens Publishing
2544 Clinton Street
Buffalo, NY 14224

Designer: Claire Wrazin
Editor: Natalie Humphrey

Photo credits: Cover, p. 1 Vitaliy6447/Shutterstock.com; background (series art) Romashka2/Shutterstock.com; p. 5 maya_parf/Shutterstock.com; p. 7 Jeff Rotman/Alamy Stock Photo; p. 9 Greens and Blues/Shutterstock.com; p. 11 Antonio Martin/iStock; p. 13 Ethan Daniels/Shutterstock.com; p. 15 Yann hubert/Shutterstock.com; p. 17 Laura Dts/Shutterstock.com; p. 19 Kim_Briers/Shutterstock.com; p. 21 Ivanva/Shutterstock.com.

Printed in the United States of America

CPSIA compliance information: Batch #CW24GS: For further information contact Gareth Stevens, New York, New York at 1-800-542-2595.

Find us on

CONTENTS

Boldface words appear in the glossary.

One Shocking Ray

A close cousin to sharks, rays are a special kind of fish. Instead of using fins to get through the water, they use round wings! But some rays are even more special. They can make **electricity**! These rays are called electric rays.

What They Look Like

Electric rays look like other rays. Their flat bodies can be brown or brightly colored with spots. They have long, skinny tails. Electric rays come in different sizes. The biggest electric rays are Atlantic torpedo rays. They can be up to 6 feet (2 m) long.

Making Electricity

To make electricity, an electric ray has an **organ** on both sides of its head. The organ is shaped like a disk. It's called a bioelectric organ. It's made of **muscle** cells called electrocytes. These cells work together to make electricity!

A Strong Charge

How strong is an electric ray's charge? Scientists measure electrical **energy** in volts. Larger rays have stronger charges. The strongest electric ray can make around 220 volts of electricity. Smaller rays make only around 37 volts.

Sensing Dinner

Electric rays use electricity when they're hunting for food! They usually hunt at night. They hide themselves on the ocean floor and wait for food to swim by. Then, when their **prey** gets close, they strike!

A Shocking Hug

To shock its dinner, an electric ray first **wraps** its body around it. Then, the ray uses its electric organs to shock the prey. When the prey isn't moving anymore, the ray opens its mouth wide to swallow the fish whole.

What's for Dinner?

Electric rays are carnivores, which means they only eat meat! They eat different meat based on their size. Smaller rays eat worms, smaller fish, and small **crustaceans**. Larger rays eat larger fish and will even eat small sharks such as dogfish!

Stay Away!

Electric rays also use their electricity to keep themselves safe. If a predator touches an electric ray, the electric ray will shock the predator to make it leave. The shock isn't enough to kill a human, but it would be enough to hurt!

Electric Medicine

Even though the chance of a shock from an electric ray keeps people away today, that wasn't always true! In **ancient** Greece and Rome, people used the shock from electric rays as **medicine**. The Greeks and Romans believed shocks from the ray could help **headaches**!

GLOSSARY

ancient: The people, places, and cultures that lived in the past.

crustacean: An animal with a hard shell, jointed limbs, feelers, and no backbone, such as a shrimp or crab.

electricity: A kind of energy that flows and is made by the movements of animals.

energy: Power used to do work.

headache: Having to do with aches or pains in the head.

medicine: A drug or treatment used to make a sick person well.

muscle: One of the parts of the body that allow movement.

organ: A part inside an animal's body.

prey: An animal that is hunted by other animals for food.

wrap: To surround or cover something with something else.

FOR MORE INFORMATION

BOOKS

Bodden, Valerie. *Rays*. Mankato, MN: Creative Education, 2022.

Leed, Percy. *Rays: A First Look*. Minneapolis, MN: Lerner Publications, 2023.

WEBSITES

Australian Museum: Short-tail Torpedo Ray

www.australian.museum/learn/animals/fishes/short-tail-torpedo-ray-torpedo-macneilli-whitley-1932/

Discover more about electric rays with pictures and maps of where they are found.

Pacific Electric Ray

www.montereybayaquarium.org/animals/animals-a-to-z/pacific-electric-ray

Read more about this kind of electric ray!

INDEX